The Human Body: Organs and Functions

LUNGS

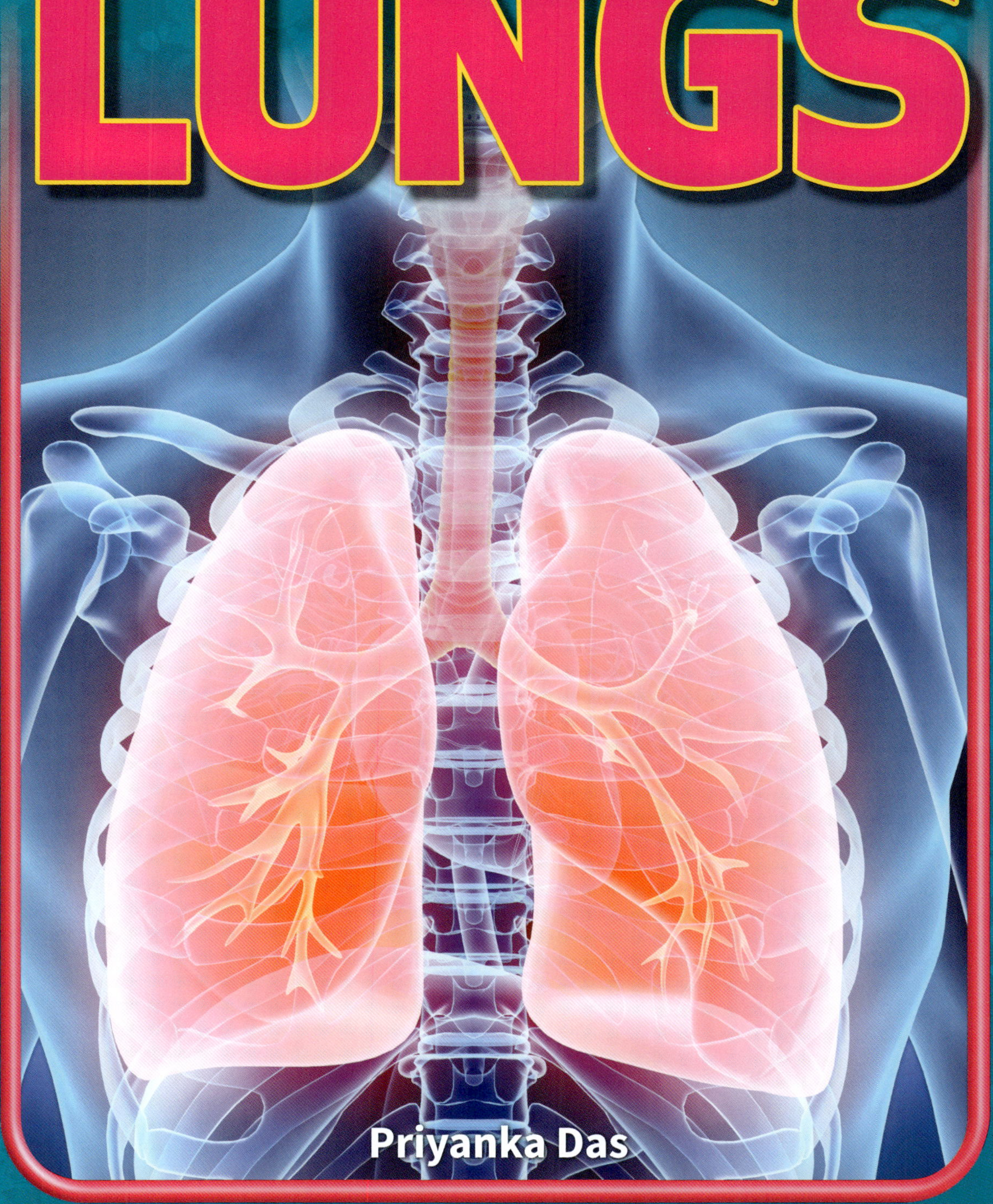

Priyanka Das

LIGHTBOX
openlightbox.com

LIGHTBOX

Go to
www.openlightbox.com
and enter this book's
unique code.

ACCESS CODE

LBXR8586

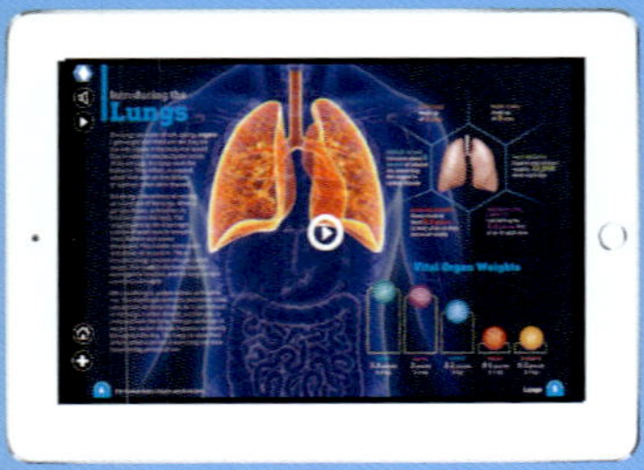

Lightbox is an all-inclusive digital solution for the teaching and learning of curriculum topics in an original, groundbreaking way. Lightbox is based on National Curriculum Standards.

LIGHTBOX SUPPLEMENTARY RESOURCES

SHARE
Share titles within your Learning Management System (LMS) or Library Circulation System

CURRICULUM
Find national and state curriculum correlations

CITATION
Create bibliographical references following APA, CMOS, and MLA styles

STANDARD FEATURES OF LIGHTBOX

AUDIO High-quality narration using text-to-speech system

ACTIVITIES Printable PDFs that can be emailed and graded

SLIDESHOWS Pictorial overviews of key concepts

VIDEOS Embedded high-definition video clips

WEBLINKS Curated links to external, child-safe resources

TRANSPARENCIES Step-by-step layering of maps, diagrams, charts, and timelines

INTERACTIVE MAPS Interactive maps and aerial satellite imagery

QUIZZES Ten multiple-choice questions that are automatically graded and emailed for teacher assessment

KEY WORDS Matching key concepts to their definitions

This title is part of our Lightbox digital subscription

Lightbox Grades 6–8 Subscription
ISBN 978-1-5105-6068-0

Access hundreds of Lightbox titles with our digital subscription. Sign up for a **FREE** subscription trial at **www.openlightbox.com/trial**

The digital components of this book are guaranteed to stay active for at least five years from the date of publication.

The Human Body: Organs and Functions

LUNGS

CONTENTS

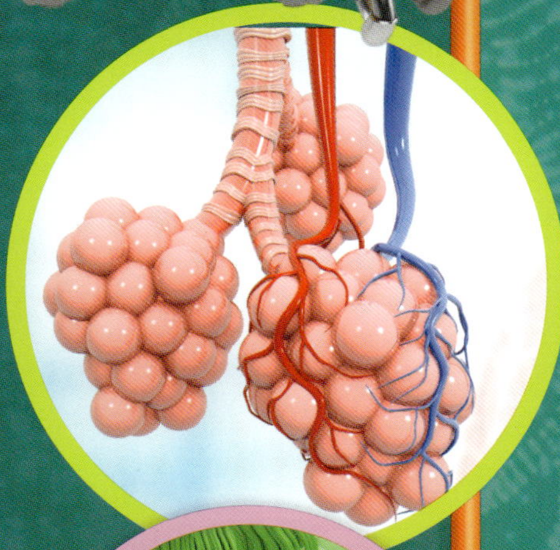

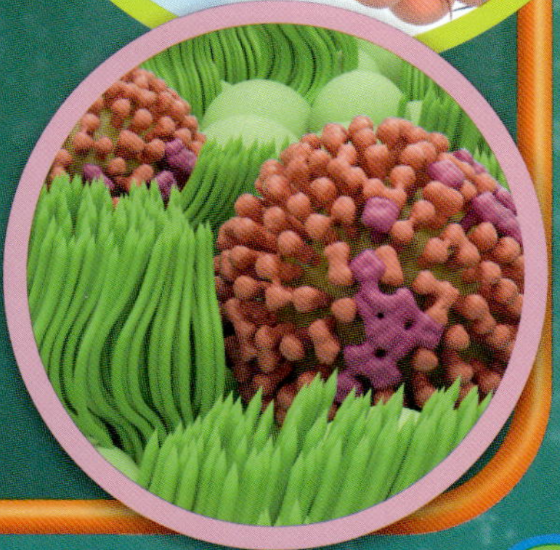

Introducing the

Lungs

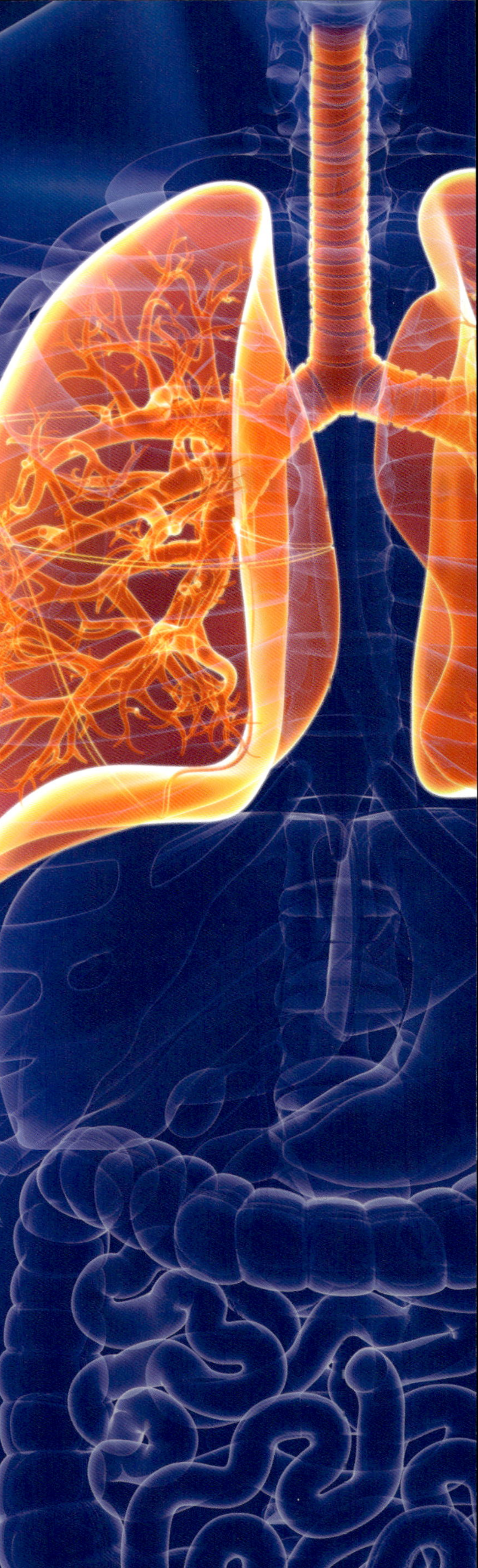

The lungs are a pair of soft, spongy **organs**. They are lightweight and are the only organs in the body that would float in water. Protected by the bones of the rib cage, the lungs work like balloons. They inflate, or expand, when filled with air and deflate, or contract, when air is released.

Breathing is the process of moving air in and out of the lungs. When a person inhales, or breathes in, fresh air enters the body. The lungs expand as the diaphragm, a dome-shaped muscle beneath them, flattens and moves downward. This creates more space and allows air to rush in. The air includes a large amount of a gas called oxygen. Every **cell** in the body depends on oxygen to function, and the lungs ensure a continuous supply.

After breathing in, people exhale, or breathe out. The diaphragm relaxes and moves back upward into its dome shape. Air is pushed out of the lungs, expelling another gas, carbon dioxide, from the body. This gas exchange of oxygen for carbon dioxide happens constantly throughout the day. The lungs increase their activity when a person is exercising and slow down during periods of rest.

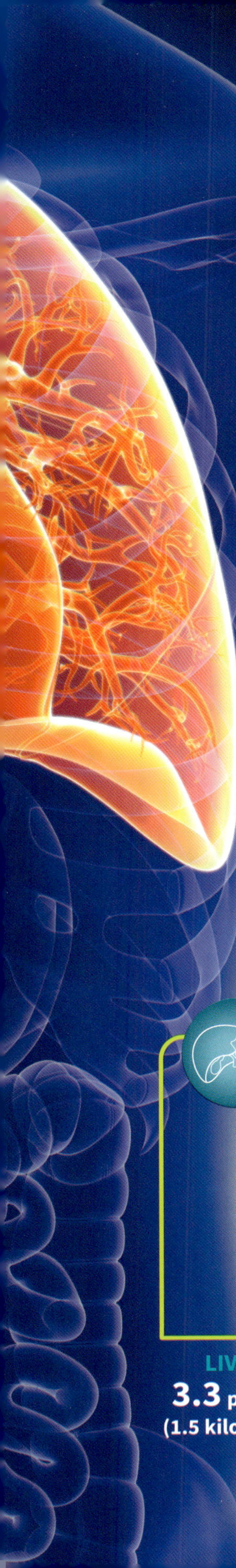

RIGHT LUNG
Made up of **3** lobes

LEFT LUNG
Made up of **2** lobes

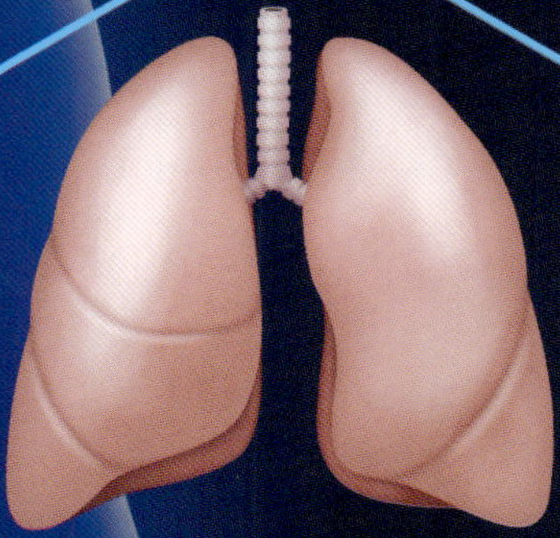

BREATHING IN
Absorb about **5** percent of inhaled air

DAILY BREATHS
Expand and contract roughly **22,000** times each day

RESIDUAL VOLUME
Always hold at least **0.3** gallons (1 liter) of air so they are never empty

MAXIMUM LUNG CAPACITY
Can hold up to **1.6** gallons (6 L) of air in adult men

Vital Organ Weights

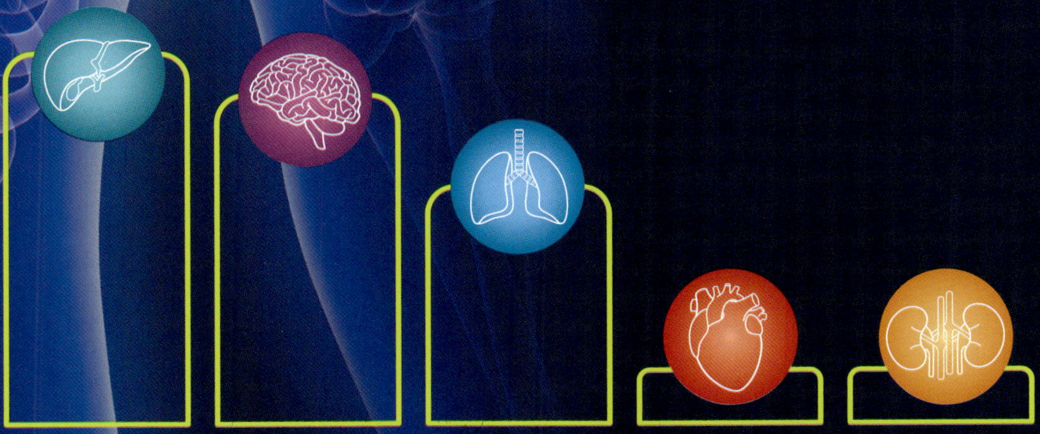

LIVER	BRAIN	LUNGS	HEART	KIDNEYS
3.3 pounds (1.5 kilograms)	**3** pounds (1.4 kg)	**2.2** pounds (1 kg)	**0.6** pounds (0.3 kg)	**0.5** pounds (0.2 kg)

The Body's Organ Systems

The lungs are part of the respiratory system. This is one of the 11 major organ systems in the human body. Each organ system is made up of multiple organs that work together to perform related tasks. Organs in turn are composed of tissues, or groups of cells that function as a unit.

Cells use oxygen to produce energy through a process called cellular respiration. This process produces carbon dioxide as a waste product. The respiratory system is responsible for bringing oxygen into the body and removing carbon dioxide from the blood. It works closely with the circulatory system to keep the body supplied with oxygen.

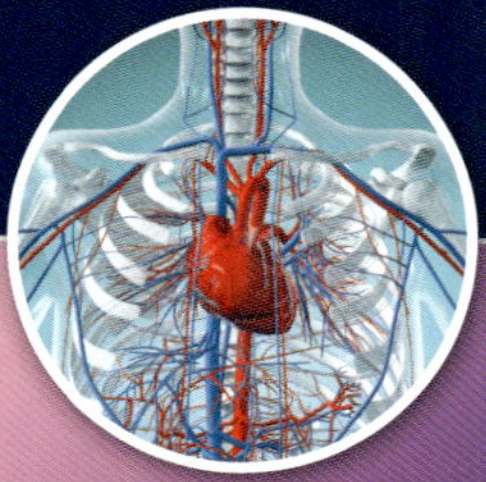

Circulatory System
Transports blood, moving substances to and from the body's cells

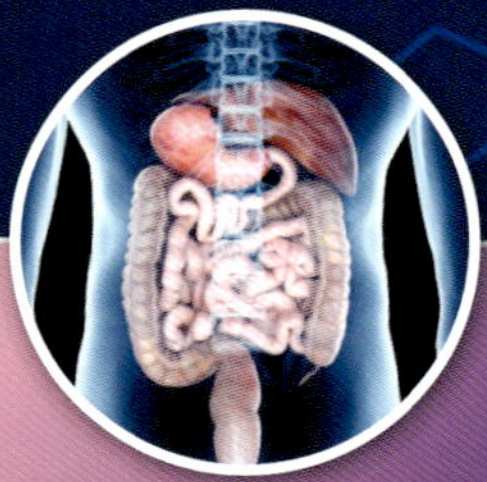

Digestive System
Extracts energy and nutrients from food

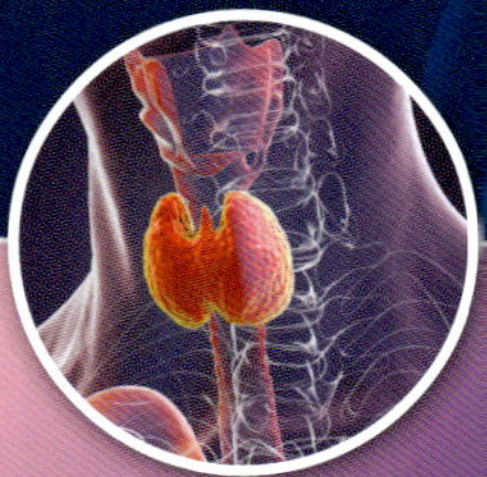

Endocrine System
Controls the release of **hormones** and maintains **homeostasis**

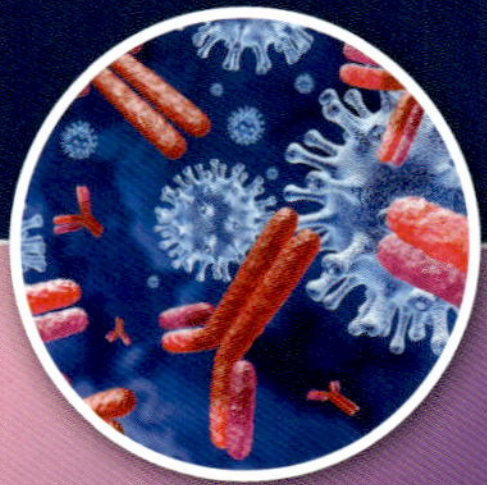

Immune System
Protects the body from attack by **pathogens**

Integumentary System
Protects the internal organs and is primarily made up of skin

Muscular System
Works together with the skeletal system to allow the body to move

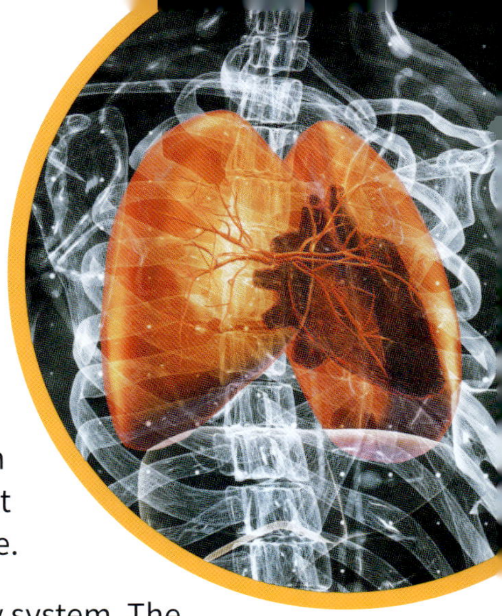

Air enters the lungs and moves into tiny sacs called alveoli. Surrounding each alveolus is a network of capillaries, the body's smallest **blood vessels**. Oxygen moves from the alveoli into the blood, while carbon dioxide passes from the blood into the alveoli. The heart, which is the central organ of the circulatory system, then pumps the oxygen-rich blood to cells throughout the body while bringing blood that holds carbon dioxide back to the lungs, completing the cycle.

The muscular and nervous systems also help the respiratory system. The diaphragm and other muscles that enable the chest cavity to expand and contract are part of the muscular system. Breathing is regulated in part by the nervous system. For example, during exercise, the brain detects higher carbon dioxide levels in the blood and signals the respiratory system to breathe faster.

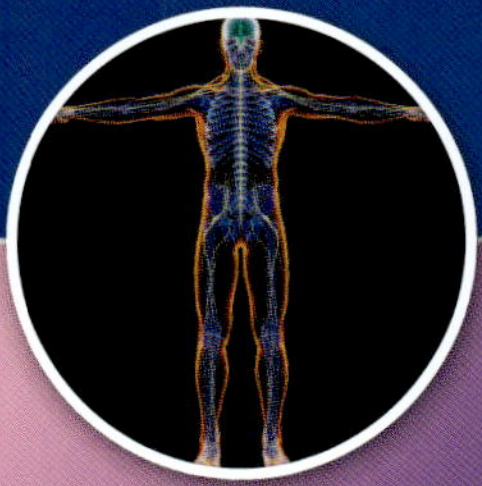

Nervous System
Carries signals between the brain and the rest of the body

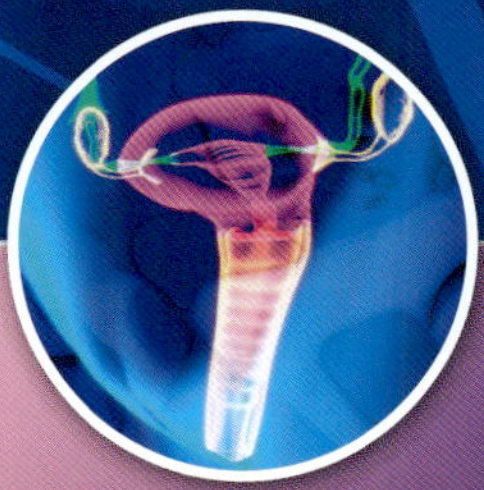

Reproductive System
Enables people to have children

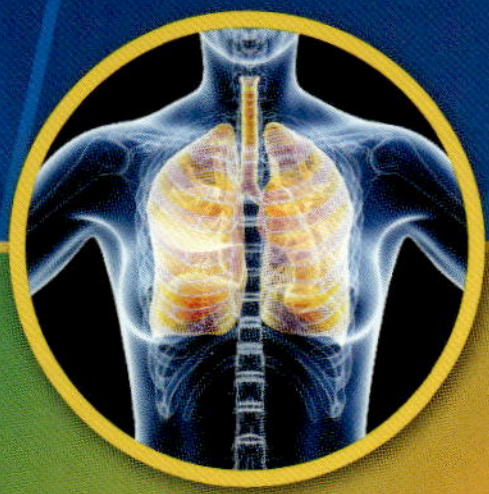

Respiratory System
Removes carbon dioxide from the body and takes in oxygen

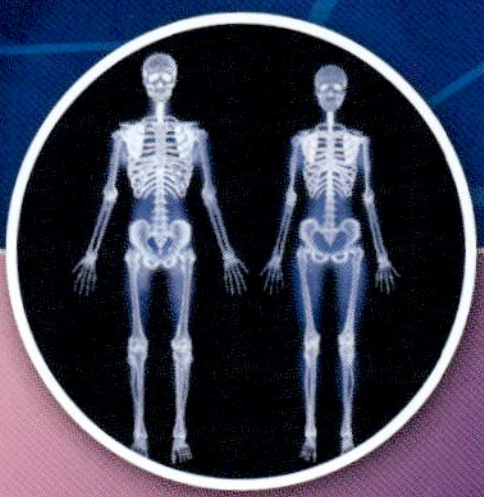

Skeletal System
Supports the body and protects the internal organs

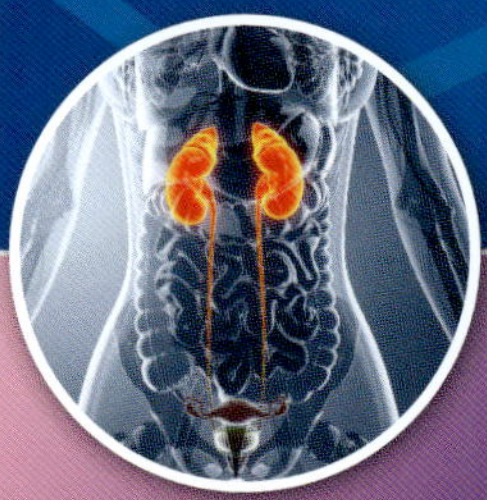

Urinary System
Filters blood, removing excess water and some waste products

Structure of the Lungs

The lungs fill up most of the space in the chest cavity. They sit on either side of the heart. The right lung is slightly larger than the left. This is because the heart leans toward the left side of the chest, taking up space where the left lung would otherwise be. Special blood vessels connect the heart and lungs, allowing them to support each other's functions.

Together, the lungs and the other organs of the respiratory system make up the respiratory tract. Breathing begins when air is drawn in through the nose or mouth. The air then travels through the upper respiratory tract, which includes the nose, nasal cavity, sinuses, pharynx, or throat, and larynx, or voice box. These structures filter, warm, and moisten the air before it continues on into the lower respiratory tract.

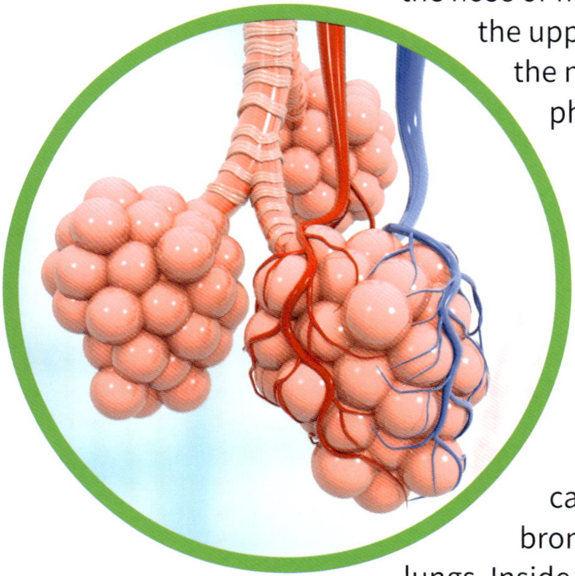

In the lower respiratory tract, air passes through the trachea, or windpipe, and into two large tubes called the bronchi. Each bronchus enters one of the lungs. Inside the lungs, the bronchi divide into smaller and smaller tubes called bronchioles, which finally end in the alveoli.

Each lung contains about 300 to 500 million alveoli. These sacs resemble clusters of grapes and provide a massive surface area for gas exchange. If all the alveoli in both of a person's lungs were spread out flat, they would cover nearly the same area as a tennis court.

Respiratory Tract

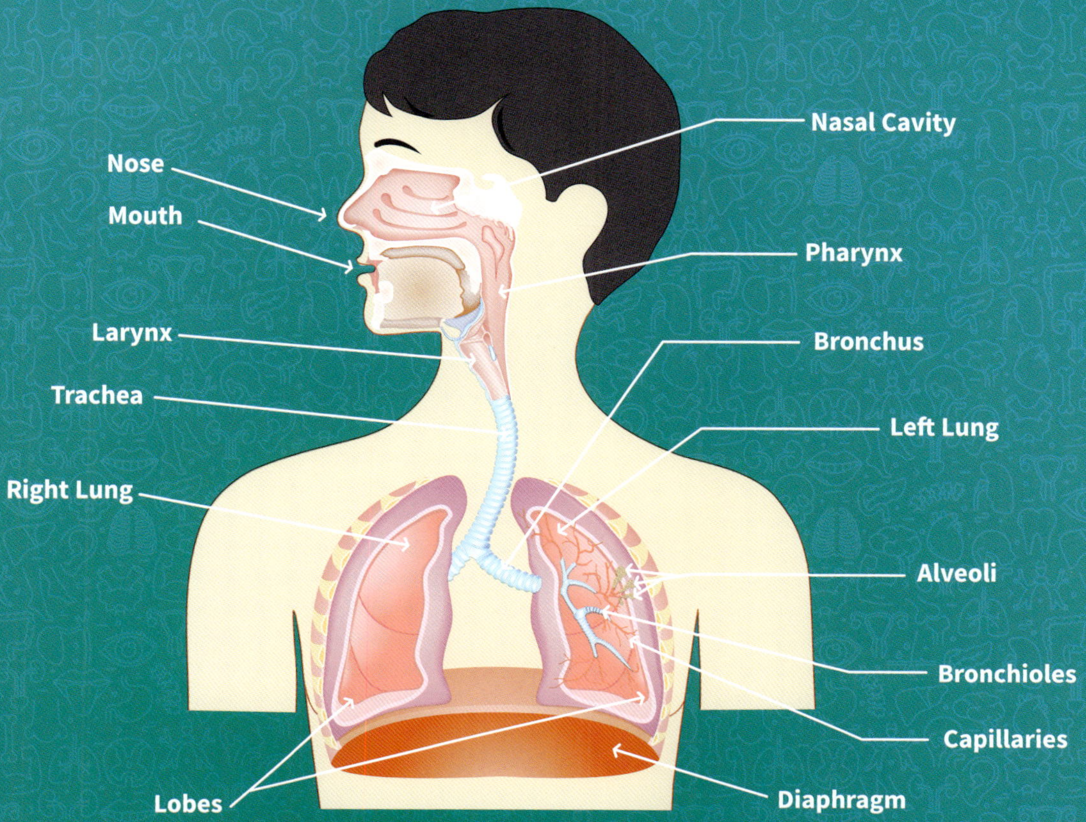

Alveoli and Gas Exchange

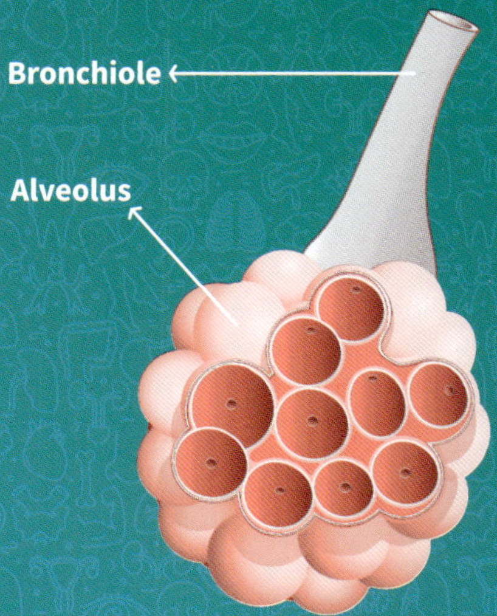

ALVEOLI

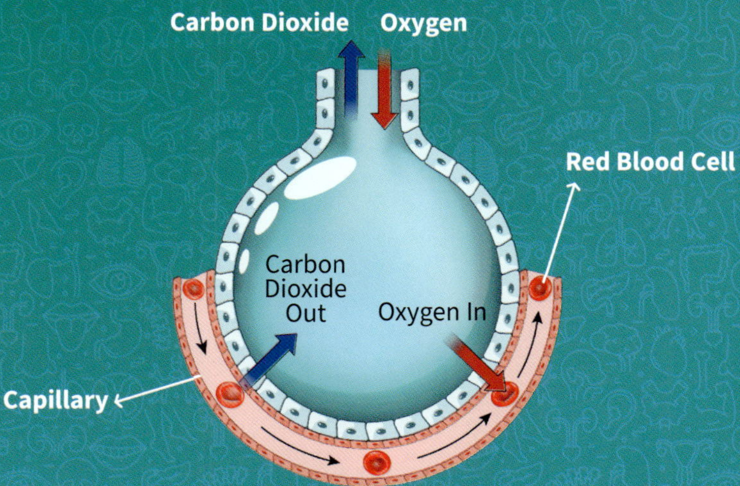

GAS EXCHANGE IN AN ALVEOLUS

Role in the Body

Under extreme conditions, it is possible to live for days without water and weeks without food. Without oxygen, however, the human body cannot survive for more than a few minutes. The lungs and the rest of the respiratory system ensure that the body has enough oxygen to meet its energy needs.

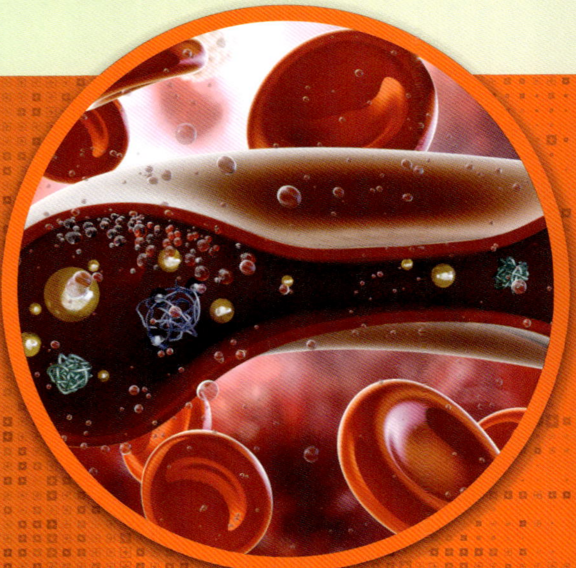

Taking in Oxygen

Oxygen makes up roughly 21 percent of the air in the atmosphere, which is the air a person inhales. The lungs consume about 5 percent of inhaled air and exhale out the rest. The only gas that they absorb from the air is oxygen. As a result, exhaled air consists of about 16 percent oxygen. The consumed oxygen is passed from the alveoli into the blood. **Hemoglobin** in red blood cells binds with oxygen, carrying it to the rest of the body.

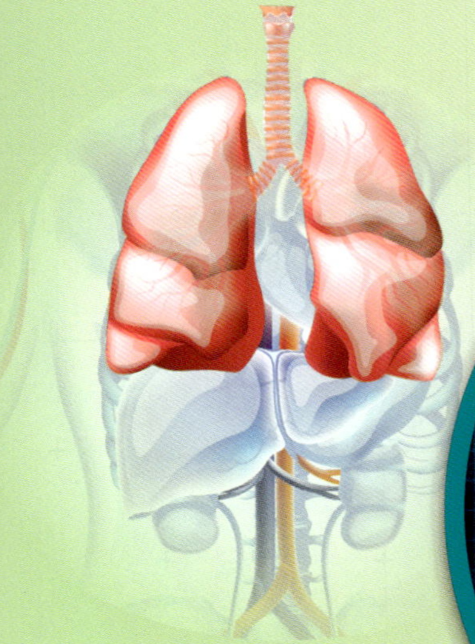

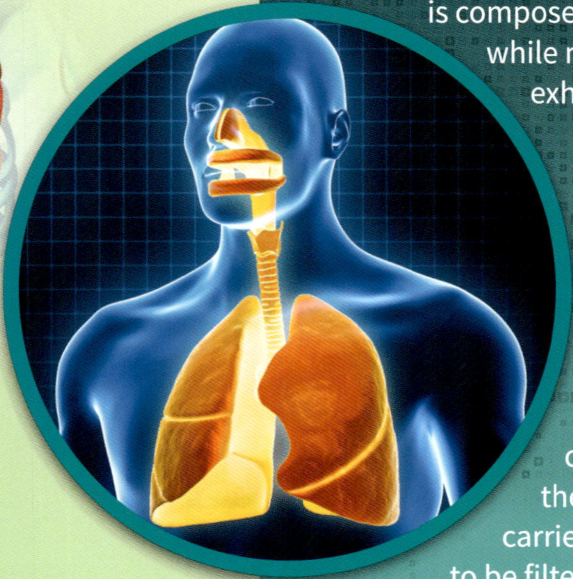

Removing Carbon Dioxide

Only 0.04 percent of air in the atmosphere is composed of carbon dioxide, while more than 4 percent of exhaled air consists of this gas. When cells use up oxygen and **glucose** for energy during cellular respiration, carbon dioxide and water are produced as byproducts. Since the body does not need carbon dioxide, it enters the bloodstream and is carried back to the lungs to be filtered out.

Protecting Against Pathogens

The respiratory system contains specialized defenses against pathogens and other harmful substances. **Mucus** in the respiratory tract traps dust, pollen, and germs, helping protect the lungs. Tiny hair-like structures called cilia line many parts of the respiratory tract. They sweep mucus and trapped particles upward to be coughed out or swallowed. Immune cells in lung tissue attack invading pathogens before they can cause infection.

Supporting Speech and Sound

The lungs play an important role in creating sounds. Air moving up from the lungs during exhalation passes through the larynx, making the vocal cords vibrate. These vibrations produce almost all human sounds, from speaking, singing, and laughing to coughing, which clears the airways.

Can You Live Without It? NO!

The brain, heart, lungs, kidneys, and liver are the five vital organs in the human body. These are the organs that the body needs in order to live. Without functioning lungs, the body cannot obtain oxygen or eliminate carbon dioxide. This leads to rapid failure of all the body's other organs as well. While people can live with partial lung function or with one lung, complete lung failure requires **mechanical ventilation** or a lung **transplant**.

A Medical Timeline

Over the centuries, scientists and physicians have made important discoveries about how the lungs work. Today, lung health can be monitored and treated more effectively than ever before. The branch of medicine that focuses on lungs is called pulmonology, from the Latin word *pulmo*, or "lung," and the Greek word *logia*, or "study."

circa 3000 BC

Ancient Egyptians draw detailed diagrams of the respiratory tract.

circa 350 BC

Greek philosopher **Aristotle** observes and compares animals with lungs and animals with gills.

circa 200 AD

Roman physician **Galen** describes the lungs as "soft and warm." He also notes that they are "kept in constant motion."

1661

Marcello Malpighi, an Italian physician, **discovers alveoli** using a microscope.

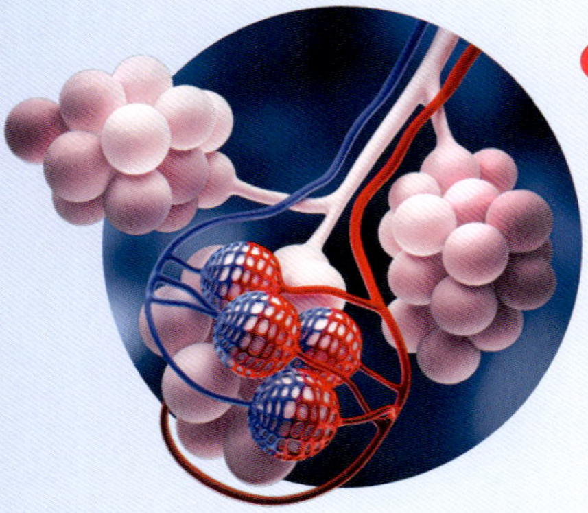

1774

English chemist Joseph Priestley **discovers oxygen**. This helps scientists understand why breathing is essential for life.

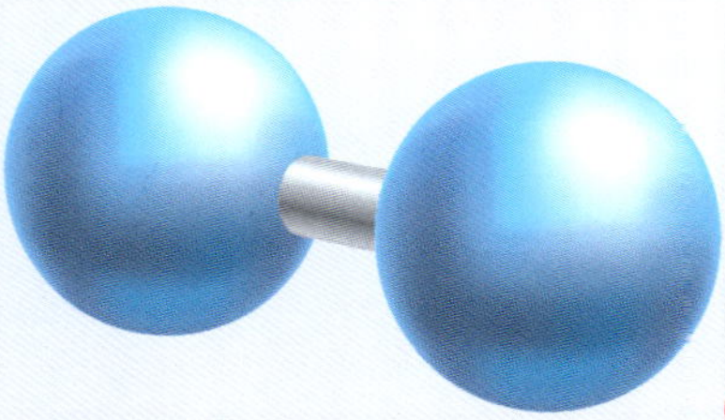

1816

The **stethoscope** is invented by French physician René Laennec. This instrument allows doctors to listen to lung sounds to detect problems.

1928

Scottish physician Alexander Fleming **discovers penicillin**, the first **antibiotic**. It helps treat **bacterial** lung infections.

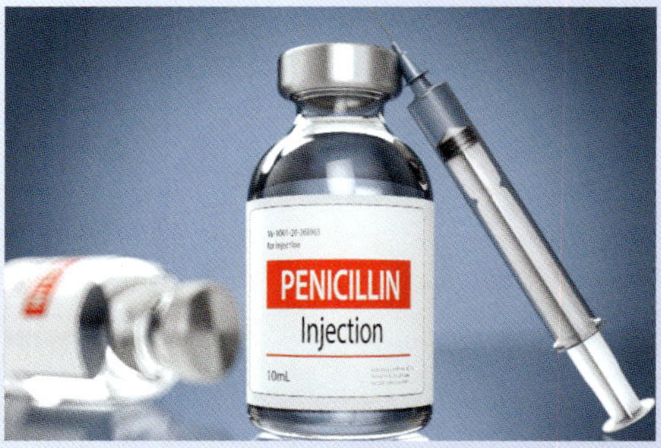

2002

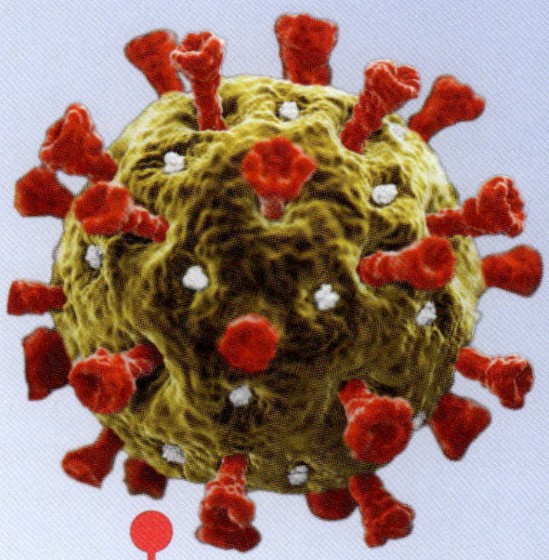

The outbreak of a respiratory infection called **severe acute respiratory syndrome (SARS)** leads to better understanding of how lung **viruses** spread between people.

2020

COVID-19 becomes a **global pandemic**. Scientists rapidly develop vaccines against this new respiratory virus.

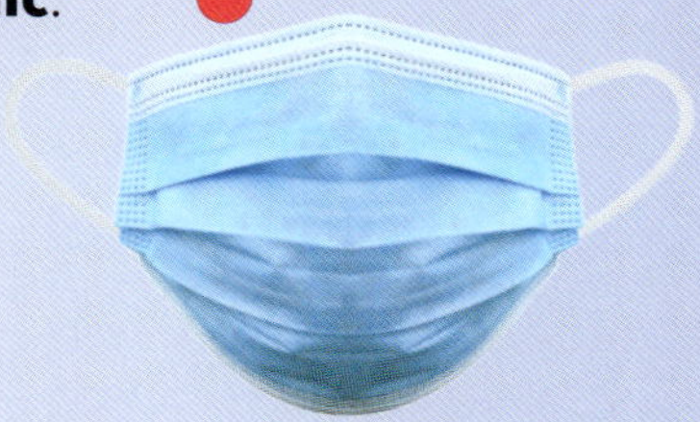

2025

Researchers continue working on developing **artificial lungs** to help patients waiting for transplants breathe more easily.

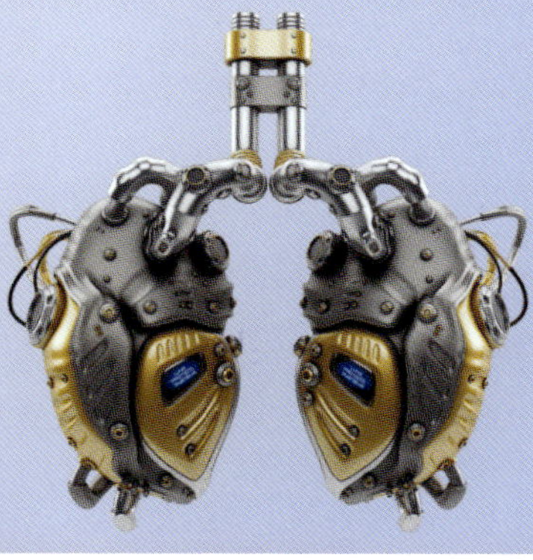

Organs Working Together

Like most organs, the lungs and the muscles that support them send signals to and receive instructions from the brain. Additionally, the lungs depend on the heart and blood vessels to help move gases. In turn, the lungs provide the rest of the body's organs with the oxygen needed for all their tasks.

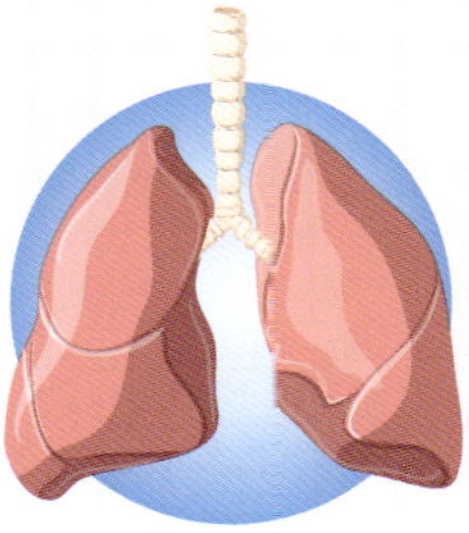

The Lungs work with the...

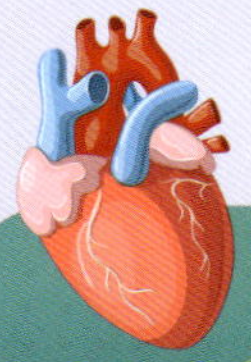

Heart to Exchange Gases

- Air enters lungs
- Oxygen moves from alveoli into blood
- Blood travels to heart through pulmonary **vein**
- Heart pumps oxygen-rich blood throughout body

- Blood carrying carbon dioxide returns to heart
- Heart sends this blood to lungs through pulmonary **artery**
- Carbon dioxide is transferred from blood to alveoli
- Carbon dioxide is exhaled out

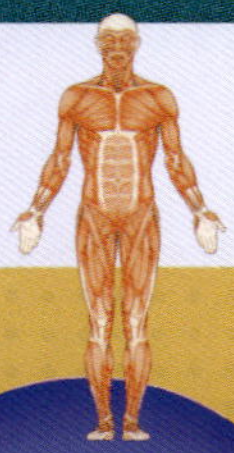

Muscles to Support Movement

- Lungs send oxygen-rich blood to heart
- Heart pumps oxygen-rich blood through blood vessels
- Blood carries oxygen to muscles
- Muscles use oxygen to create energy for movement

Brain to Control Breathing

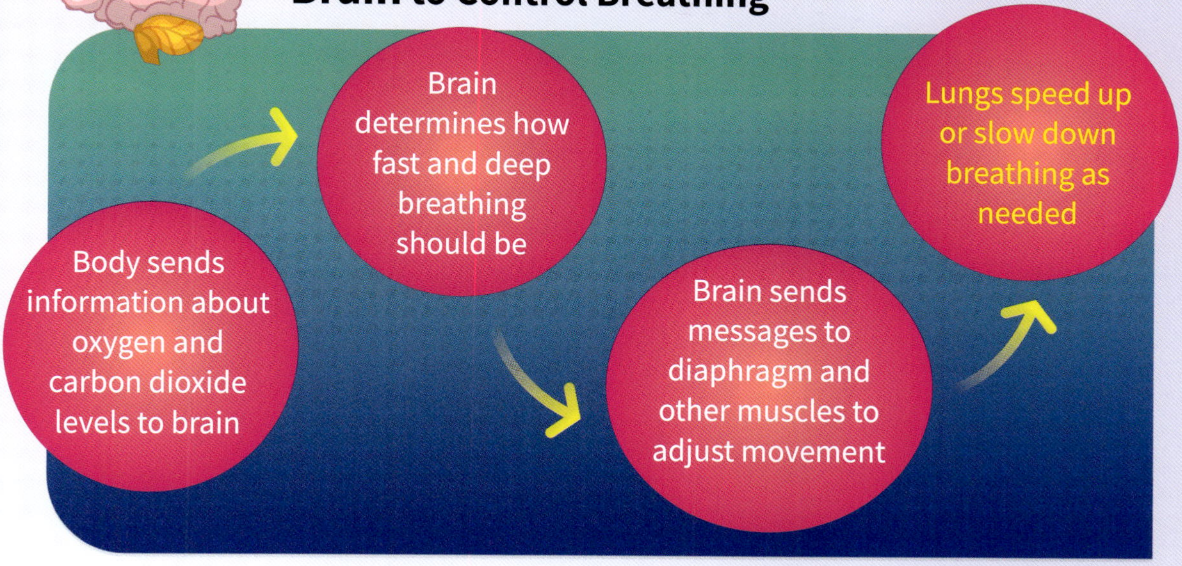

Diaphragm to Make Breathing Possible

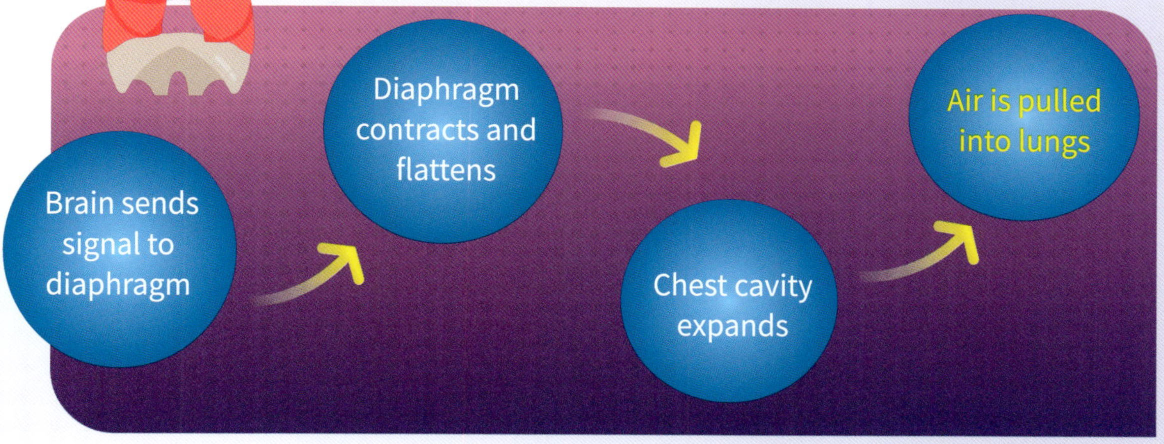

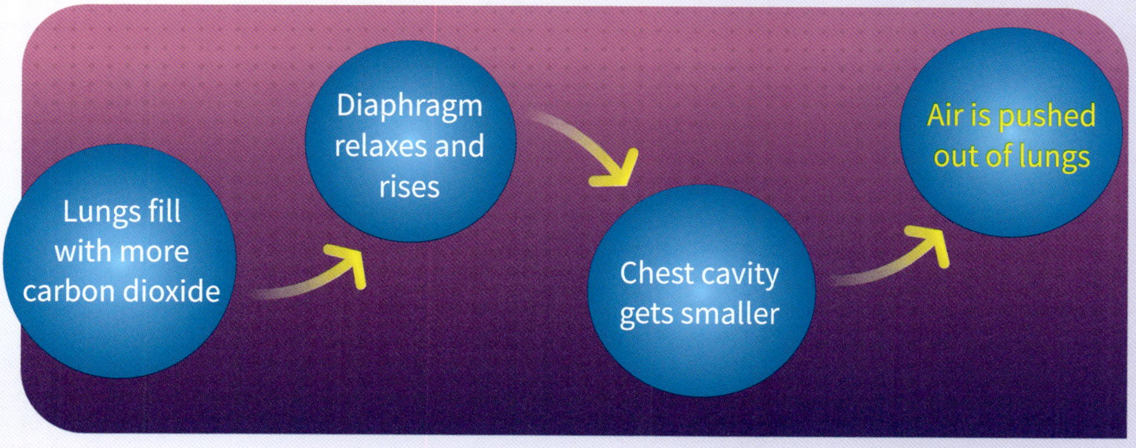

Diseases of the Lungs

Several serious conditions can affect lung function and breathing. Asthma, pneumonia, chronic obstructive pulmonary disease (COPD), and lung cancer are some examples. These conditions may damage lung tissue, block airways, or prevent proper oxygen exchange.

Asthma

Asthma causes **inflammation** and narrowing of the airways, or passages in the respiratory tract. During an asthma attack, the airways swell and produce extra mucus, making breathing difficult. Some common causes of asthma attacks include **allergies**, intense exercise, cold air, and pollution. Asthma cannot be cured but can be managed with medication.

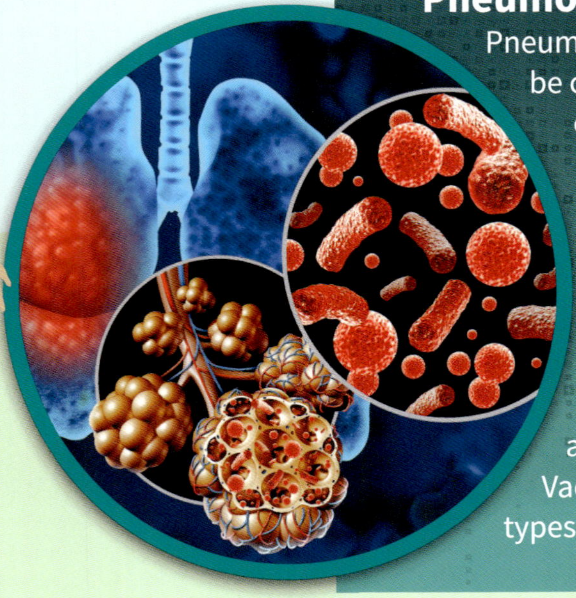

Pneumonia

Pneumonia is an infection that can be caused by bacteria, viruses, or fungi, which include organisms such as mold. This infection inflames the alveoli in one or both lungs. The alveoli may fill with fluid or pus. Symptoms of pneumonia include cough, fever, and difficulty breathing. Vaccines help prevent some types of bacterial pneumonia.

Chronic Obstructive Pulmonary Disease

COPD is a progressive disease that makes breathing increasingly difficult. Its two main forms are chronic bronchitis and emphysema. Chronic bronchitis develops from repeated inflammation of the airways, while emphysema refers to damaged alveoli. Smoking is the leading cause of COPD.

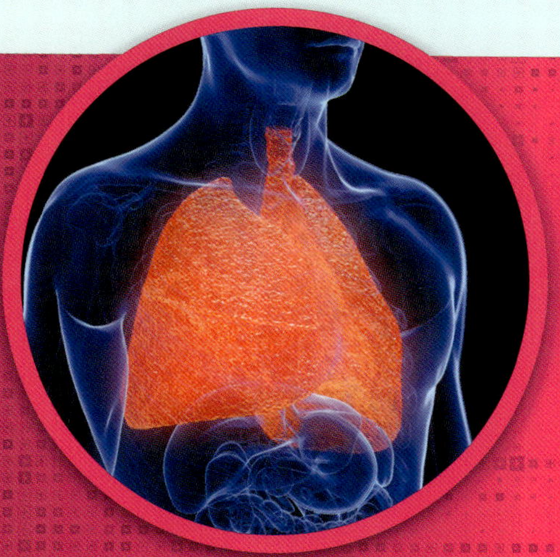

Lung Cancer

Lung cancer occurs when abnormal cells grow uncontrollably in lung tissue, forming masses called tumors. These tumors can block airways and spread to other organs. Lung cancer usually begins in the bronchi, bronchioles, or alveoli. It then spreads to the rest of the lung and to other organs.

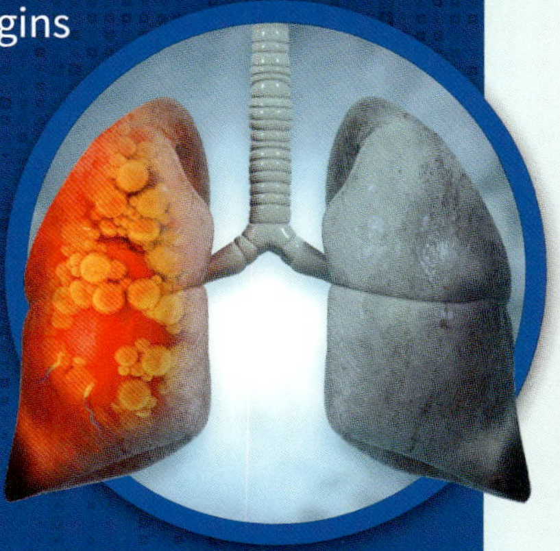

Warning Signs!

Lung diseases often develop gradually. However, there are some symptoms to watch out for. If these signs appear, it is important to go to a doctor right away.

- Persistent cough lasting weeks
- Shortness of breath during routine activities
- Wheezing or whistling sound when breathing
- Coughing up blood
- Excessive mucus
- Chest pain that worsens with breathing
- Frequent respiratory infections

Healthy Lungs vs. Smoker's Lungs

Smoking is one of the most damaging habits for lung health. Healthy lungs should be pinkish-gray in color with tissue that is smooth, elastic, and expands easily with each breath. A smoker's lungs develop black spots and dark discoloration. The tissue becomes stiff and less flexible, while the airways swell and produce excess mucus. Over time, smoking destroys alveoli, creating large air pockets that reduce oxygen absorption.

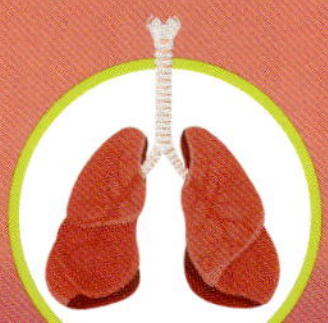

Healthy Lungs

- Pinkish-Gray
- Smooth Tissue
- Normal Size
- Dome-Shaped Diaphragm

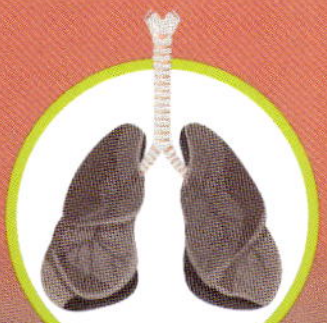

Smoker's Lungs

- Gray to Black
- Inflamed Patches
- Expanded Size due to Trapped Air
- Muscle Loss in Diaphragm

Medicine around the World

Lung diseases affect millions of people around the world. A number of hospitals, research centers, and universities focus on studying lung diseases and developing new ways to prevent, diagnose, and treat them. Some of these institutions are known internationally for their work in respiratory care, surgery, and lung transplants.

1 National Jewish Health, United States

Located in Denver, Colorado, National Jewish Health is one of the top U.S. centers for respiratory care and research. It specializes in treating diseases such as asthma, COPD, **cystic fibrosis**, and **interstitial lung disease**. The center is also known for its research into immune system disorders that affect the lungs.

2 Royal Brompton Hospital, United Kingdom

Royal Brompton Hospital, in London, is among Europe's best-known hospitals for lung and heart diseases. It is known for its work in respiratory infections, cystic fibrosis, and lung transplantation. The hospital is also a major center for children with lung conditions and runs one of the largest lung research programs in the United Kingdom.

University of Cape Town Lung Institute, South Africa

3

The University of Cape Town Lung Institute (UCTLI) is well known for its research into asthma, smoking-related lung disease, and **tuberculosis**. It works to improve lung health in South Africa and across the African continent. The institute also focuses on researching and treating childhood respiratory illnesses.

Christian Medical College, India

4

Christian Medical College (CMC), located in Vellore, is a leading university hospital in India that treats lung infections such as tuberculosis. India has the highest number of tuberculosis cases in the world, making up more than 25 percent worldwide. CMC also trains doctors in respiratory medicine and provides care for asthma, lung injuries, and other breathing disorders.

What is a Pulmonologist?

Pulmonologists are doctors who specialize in lung and respiratory system diseases. They diagnose and treat asthma, bronchitis, cystic fibrosis, and tuberculosis, among other conditions. Tools including x-rays, CT scans, and lung function tests help pulmonologists diagnose lung problems. Many pulmonologists provide care for patients who need machines, such as ventilators, to help them breathe.

Keeping the Lungs Healthy

People can practice healthy habits to protect their lungs. Good hygiene, regular exercise, and avoiding harmful substances help keep the respiratory system functioning well. Vaccines are also available to prevent some lung diseases.

TIP 1

Stay Active
Activities such as running, swimming, and cycling strengthen the lungs by improving oxygen intake.

TIP 2

Breathe Clean Air
Polluted air may come from traffic, factories, or wildfire smoke. Avoid areas with heavy smoke or air pollution.

TIP 3

Stay Away from Smoking and Vaping
Smoking is a leading cause of lung disease. It damages the airways and makes it harder to breathe. Breathing in secondhand smoke is also harmful. Vaping can hurt the lungs as well, especially in children and teenagers.

TIP 4

Stay Up to Date on Recommended Vaccines
Vaccinations for pneumonia, whooping cough, and the flu help prevent respiratory infections that can damage the lungs.

TIP 5

Practice Good Hygiene
Washing your hands regularly and covering your mouth when coughing or sneezing helps stop the spread of viruses that affect the lungs, including colds and the flu.

Activity: Measure Your Lung Capacity

Lung capacity is the amount of air that the lungs can hold. On average, men have a larger lung capacity than women. Lung capacity also varies based on age, height, and fitness level. Try measuring your lung capacity and comparing it with that of other people.

Materials

- Round balloons of the same size
- Measuring tape
- Pen and paper

Steps

1. Prepare a Balloon: Stretch the balloon a few times to make it easier to inflate. This helps make sure it expands evenly.

2. Take a Deep Breath: Stand or sit up straight. Take a deep breath and blow one full breath into the balloon. Blow as much air as possible in one try. Then, pinch the balloon closed and tie it up to keep the air inside.

3. Measure the Balloon: Wrap the measuring tape around the widest part of the balloon to measure its circumference. Record the number in inches or centimeters.

4. Repeat and Compare: Try the activity three times, resting between each try. Use the largest measurement as your final result. Compare results with your friends or classmates or try the activity again after some light exercise to see if there are any changes.

5. Discussion: Larger balloon sizes mean more air was exhaled, showing higher lung capacity. Deep breathing exercises and physical activity can help the lungs grow stronger over time. You can repeat the test monthly to track any changes in lung capacity.

Quiz

1
Which organ system are the lungs part of?

2
What are the tiny air sacs in the lungs known as?

3
Oxygen makes up what percentage of the air in the atmosphere?

4
What is breathing?

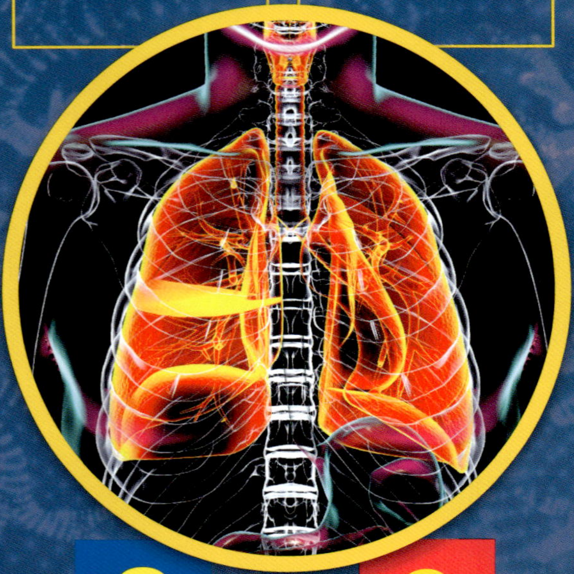

5
Who discovered oxygen?

6
Is the left lung or the right lung larger?

7
What is the pharynx also called?

8
Which dome-shaped muscle helps expand and contract the chest cavity?

9
What is pneumonia?

10
Which process in the body produces carbon dioxide as a waste product?

ANSWERS
1. Respiratory system **2.** Alveoli **3.** 21 percent **4.** The process of moving air in and out of the lungs **5.** English chemist Joseph Priestley **6.** Right lung **7.** Throat **8.** Diaphragm **9.** An infection that inflames the alveoli in one or both lungs **10.** Cellular espiration

Key Words

allergies: immune system reactions to substances such as pollen, food, or dust that are normally harmless

antibiotic: a type of medicine used to treat bacterial infections

artery: a blood vessel that carries blood away from the heart

bacterial: relating to tiny single-celled organisms known as bacteria

blood vessels: tubes, such as arteries, veins, and capillaries, that carry blood throughout the body

cell: the smallest structural and functional unit of living organisms

cystic fibrosis: a genetic disorder that causes a buildup of mucus in the body

glucose: a simple sugar that is the main source of energy for the body's cells

hemoglobin: a protein that contains iron and is found in red blood cells

homeostasis: the body's ability to maintain a stable internal environment despite external changes

hormones: chemical messengers that affect many functions in the body

inflammation: the body's response to injury or infection, often resulting in redness, swelling, heat, or pain

interstitial lung disease: a group of disorders that cause inflammation and scarring of the lungs

mechanical ventilation: the use of a machine to help a person breathe

mucus: a sticky, slippery substance produced by the body

organs: distinct structures in the body that are made up of tissues and perform one or more specific functions

pathogens: microorganisms, such as bacteria or viruses, that cause diseases

transplant: a medical procedure in which an organ or tissue is moved from one person to another, or from one part of the body to another

tuberculosis: a serious bacterial infection that mainly affects the lungs and can cause coughing, chest pain, and fever

vein: a blood vessel that carries blood to the heart

viruses: tiny infectious agents that can only multiply inside the living cells of a host organism

Index

LIGHTBOX

SUPPLEMENTARY RESOURCES

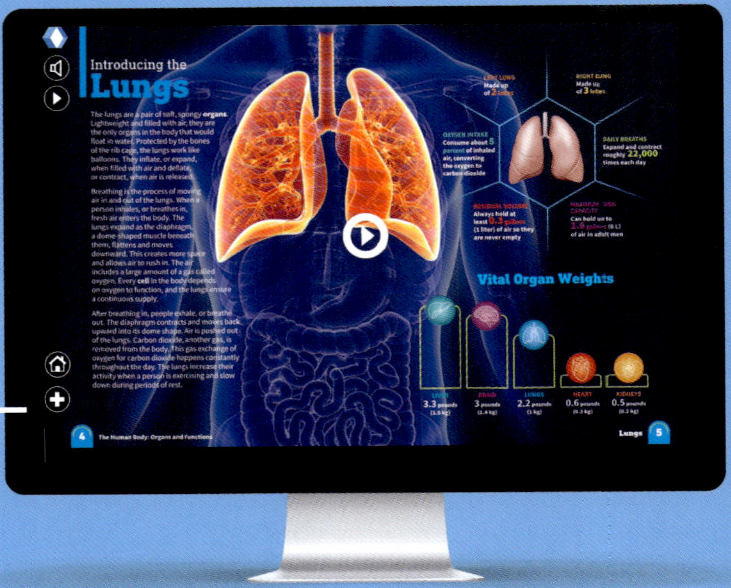

Click on the plus icon found in the bottom left corner of each spread to open additional teacher resources.

- Download and print the book's quizzes and activities
- Access curriculum correlations
- Explore additional web applications that enhance the Lightbox experience

LIGHTBOX DIGITAL TITLES

Packed full of integrated media

VIDEOS

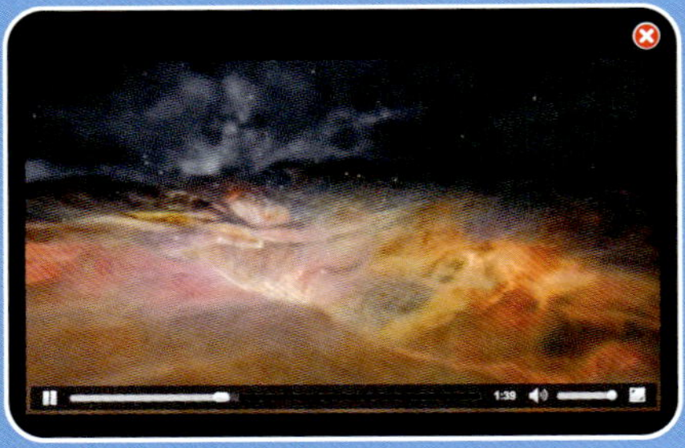

INTERACTIVE MAPS

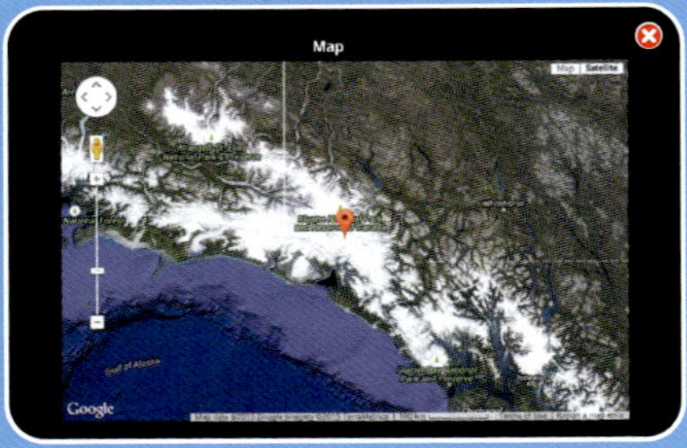

WEBLINKS

SLIDESHOWS

QUIZZES

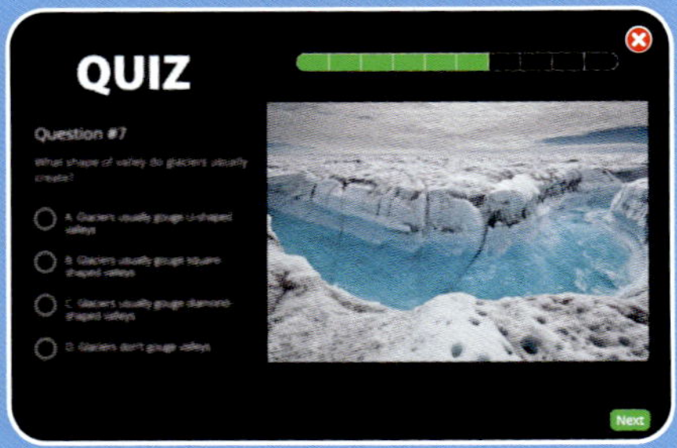

OPTIMIZED FOR

- ✔ TABLETS
- ✔ SMART BOARDS
- ✔ COMPUTERS
- ✔ AND MUCH MORE!

Published by Lightbox Learning Inc.
276 5th Avenue, Suite 704 #917
New York, NY 10001
Website: www.openlightbox.com

Library of Congress Control Number: 2025932684

ISBN 978-1-5105-8671-0 (hardcover)
ISBN 978-1-5105-8672-7 (static multi-user eBook)
ISBN 978-1-5105-8676-5 (interactive multi-user eBook)

Printed in Fargo, North Dakota, in the United States of America
2 3 4 5 6 7 8 9 0 30 29 28 27 26

012026
260119

Project Coordinator: Priyanka Das
Design: Jean Faye Rodriguez